Inventions, Inventors, & You

Written by Dianne Draze
Illustrated by Dean and Pat Crawford

First published in 2005 by Prufrock Press Inc.

Published in 2021 by Routledge
605 Third Avenue, New York, NY 10017
2 Park Square, Milton Park, Abingdon, Oxon OX14 4RN

Routledge is an imprint of the Taylor & Francis Group, an informa business

Copyright © 2005 by Taylor & Francis Group

Notice:
Product or corporate names may be trademarks or registered trademarks, and are used only for identification and explanation without intent to infringe.

ISBN: 9781593630829 (pbk)

DOI: 10.4324/9781003235880

Inventions, Inventors, You

All lessons in this book align to the following standards.

Grade Level	Common Core State Standards in ELA/Literacy
Grade 3	RI.3.3 Describe the relationship between a series of historical events, scientific ideas or concepts, or steps in technical procedures in a text, using language that pertains to time, sequence, and cause/effect. RI.3.4 Determine the meaning of general academic and domain-specific words and phrases in a text relevant to a grade 3 topic or subject area. RF.3.3 Know and apply grade-level phonics and word analysis skills in decoding words. RF.3.4 Read with sufficient accuracy and fluency to support comprehension. W.3.1 Write opinion pieces on topics or texts, supporting a point of view with reasons. W.3.2 Write informative/explanatory texts to examine a topic and convey ideas and information clearly. W.3.7 Conduct short research projects that build knowledge about a topic. W.3.8 Recall information from experiences or gather information from print and digital sources; take brief notes on sources and sort evidence into provided categories. SL.3.4 Report on a topic or text, tell a story, or recount an experience with appropriate facts and relevant, descriptive details, speaking clearly at an understandable pace.
Grade 4	RI.4.3 Explain events, procedures, ideas, or concepts in a historical, scientific, or technical text, including what happened and why, based on specific information in the text. RI.4.4 Determine the meaning of general academic and domain-specific words or phrases in a text relevant to a grade 4 topic or subject area. RF.4.3 Know and apply grade-level phonics and word analysis skills in decoding words. RF.4.4 Read with sufficient accuracy and fluency to support comprehension. W.4.1 Write opinion pieces on topics or texts, supporting a point of view with reasons and information. W.4.2 Write informative/explanatory texts to examine a topic and convey ideas and information clearly. W.4.7 Conduct short research projects that build knowledge through investigation of different aspects of a topic. W.4.8 Recall relevant information from experiences or gather relevant information from print and digital sources; take notes and categorize information, and provide a list of sources. SL.4.4 Report on a topic or text, tell a story, or recount an experience in an organized manner, using appropriate facts and relevant, descriptive details to support main ideas or themes; speak clearly at an understandable pace. SL.4.5 Add audio recordings and visual displays to presentations when appropriate to enhance the development of main ideas or themes.
Grade 5	RI.5.3 Explain the relationships or interactions between two or more individuals, events, ideas, or concepts in a historical, scientific, or technical text based on specific information in the text. RI.5.4 Determine the meaning of general academic and domain-specific words and phrases in a text relevant to a grade 5 topic or subject area. RI.5.7 Draw on information from multiple print or digital sources, demonstrating the ability to locate an answer to a question quickly or to solve a problem efficiently. RI.5.9 Integrate information from several texts on the same topic in order to write or speak about the subject knowledgeably. RF.5.3 Know and apply grade-level phonics and word analysis skills in decoding words. RF.5.4 Read with sufficient accuracy and fluency to support comprehension. W.5.1 Write opinion pieces on topics or texts, supporting a point of view with reasons and information. W.5.2 Write informative/explanatory texts to examine a topic and convey ideas and information clearly. W.5.7 Conduct short research projects that use several sources to build knowledge through investigation of different aspects of a topic. W.5.8 Recall relevant information from experiences or gather relevant information from print and digital sources; summarize or paraphrase information in notes and finished work, and provide a list of sources. SL.5.4 Report on a topic or text or present an opinion, sequencing ideas logically and using appropriate facts and relevant, descriptive details to support main ideas or themes; speak clearly at an understandable pace. SL.5.5 Include multimedia components (e.g., graphics, sound) and visual displays in presentations when appropriate to enhance the development of main ideas or themes

Common Core State Standards Alignment Sheet
Inventions, Inventors, You

All lessons in this book align to the following standards.

Grade Level	Common Core State Standards in ELA/Literacy
Grade 6	RI.6.7 Integrate information presented in different media or formats (e.g., visually, quantitatively) as well as in words to develop a coherent understanding of a topic or issue. W.6.1 Write arguments to support claims with clear reasons and relevant evidence. W.6.2 Write informative/explanatory texts to examine a topic and convey ideas, concepts, and information through the selection, organization, and analysis of relevant content. W.6.7 Conduct short research projects to answer a question, drawing on several sources and refocusing the inquiry when appropriate. W.6.8 Gather relevant information from multiple print and digital sources; assess the credibility of each source; and quote or paraphrase the data and conclusions of others while avoiding plagiarism and providing basic bibliographic information for sources. SL.6.4 Present claims and findings, sequencing ideas logically and using pertinent descriptions, facts, and details to accentuate main ideas or themes; use appropriate eye contact, adequate volume, and clear pronunciation. SL.6.5 Include multimedia components (e.g., graphics, images, music, sound) and visual displays in presentations to clarify information.
Grade 7	W.7.1 Write arguments to support claims with clear reasons and relevant evidence W.7.2 Write informative/explanatory texts to examine a topic and convey ideas, concepts, and information through the selection, organization, and analysis of relevant content. W.7.7 Conduct short research projects to answer a question, drawing on several sources and generating additional related, focused questions for further research and investigation. SL.7.4 Present claims and findings, emphasizing salient points in a focused, coherent manner with pertinent descriptions, facts, details, and examples; use appropriate eye contact, adequate volume, and clear pronunciation. SL.7.5 Include multimedia components and visual displays in presentations to clarify claims and findings and emphasize salient points.
Grades 6-8	RH.6-8.3 Identify key steps in a text's description of a process related to history/social studies (e.g., how a bill becomes law, how interest rates are raised or lowered). RH.6-8.4 Determine the meaning of words and phrases as they are used in a text, including vocabulary specific to domains related to history/social studies. RH.6-8.7 Integrate visual information (e.g., in charts, graphs, photographs, videos, or maps) with other information in print and digital texts. RH.6-8.8 Distinguish among fact, opinion, and reasoned judgment in a text. RST.6-8.10 By the end of grade 8, read and comprehend science/technical texts in the grades 6–8 text complexity band independently and proficiently. WHST.6-8.1 Write arguments focused on discipline-specific content. WHST.6-8.2 Write informative/explanatory texts to examine a topic and convey ideas, concepts, and information through the selection, organization, and analysis of relevant content. WHST.6-8.7 Conduct short research projects to answer a question, drawing on several sources and refocusing the inquiry when appropriate. WHST.6-8.8 Gather relevant information from multiple print and digital sources; assess the credibility of each source; and quote or paraphrase the data and conclusions of others while avoiding plagiarism and providing basic bibliographic information for sources. WHST.6-8.9 Draw evidence from literary or informational texts to support analysis, reflection, and research.

Introduction

Invent - *To think out or produce a new device or process—something that is needed or a better way of doing things.*

Humans are set apart from animals by their imagination. Some animals can run faster, some can fly higher, and some are stronger than humans. But only humans have been able to exercise their imaginations to reshape their environments and overcome their physical limitations. From earliest history, people have been looking for ways to make work easier. We have used our creativity to find thousands of ways to improve our existence. We have come a long way since our ancestor's first inventions — stone weapons. We now live in a technologically advanced society and have become so accustomed to continual scientific and technological advances that we take a lot of inventions for granted.

Who are the inventors? Are they some rare breed of individuals who are born with special talents? To be sure, most inventors have extensive knowledge combined with creative abilities and special personal characteristics; however, it would seem that everyone possess the inventive spirit. From a youngster's playful attempts to use objects in new ways to the adult's efforts to solve everyday problems, we see the inventive mind analyzing situations and thinking of new ways to accomplish the task at hand or to simplify our work.

We all invent. Most inventions are only attempts to help ourselves — to solve the problem facing us at that particular instant. Some inventions, on the other hand, are more noteworthy and dramatically affect civilization. Regardless of the significance of the invention, the process is similar. And this inventive process can be learned. People can be taught to be more aware of problems that need solutions, to be more creative in posing solutions, and to be meticulous about testing ideas.

Inventions, Inventors and You is a comprehensive unit that will not only acquaint students with significant inventions and inventors but will also give them techniques for being more creative and inventive. **Inventions, Inventors and You** takes invention out of the history book and brings it to life.

Inventions, Inventors and You offers something for every teaching and learning style. It provides ideas for group lessons, worksheets, learning centers and cards for individual projects. There are several concepts presented in this book, and these concepts are repeated in the lessons, worksheets, and projects. In this way, you have many options for providing reinforcement for the initial presentation.

The concepts that are presented in this book are as follows:
- Characteristics and abilities of inventors
- All developments build on previous ones
- Techniques for creative thinking
- How inventions influence our lives
- What inventions are most worthwhile
- How inventors are influenced by society and the state of technology
- Where ideas come from
- Defining and understanding creativity
- Inventions are a result of problems that need to be solved

Contents

Directed Lessons

Lesson 1—Pretest/Preview
Give pretest on inventors and inventions.
Correct pretest and discuss answers.
Make notebook to keep work in.

Lesson 2—Why Man Creates
Discuss the following questions:
  What do you want to know about inventors or inventions?
  What are some of the most important inventions?
  What is creativity?
  Are we all creative?
  If you were an invention, what would you be? Why?
  If available, view the film "Why Man Creates." This film moves very rapidly. You may want to show it to the students twice, so they can absorb and appreciate everything that is shown in the film.
Discuss the following:
  What did you see?
  What inventions were shown in the film?
  What did the inventors have to say?
  How does that make you feel?
  After viewing the film, did your ideas about creativity or inventing change?

Lesson 3—Brainstorming
  Introduce brainstorming as a techniques for coming up with new ideas by working as a group to make a long list of ideas.
  Review rules for brainstorming.
    Everyone may contribute ideas.
    All answers are accepted.
    No judgement or evaluation is offered until after the brainstorming session is over.
    Try to get as many ideas as possible.
    Piggybacking or combining ideas is encouraged.
  Present the class with the following situation:
  "Your Uncle Fred has just died, and the will states that you have inherited all of his old tires. He left these tires to you, because he felt that you are the most creative person in the family and would be able to think of good uses for these tires. He does not want them destroyed. He wants them put to good use. What will you do with all the tires?"
  Encourage a large variety of ideas. After students have listed as many ideas as possible, ask them to individually choose the three ideas that they think are the best.
  It takes practice to be able to work well as a group with brainstorming, so this might be a lesson that you would like to repeat several times. Other ideas for brainstorming are:
    In want ways might we improve bicycles?
    In what ways might we get more exercise?
    What are some ideas for making learning painless?
    What are all the uses you can think of for a pencil?
    What are some ways to improve our school yard?
    What are some ways to improve back packs?

Lesson 4—Check Lists
  Present students with a paper bag and ask them to brainstorm a list of uses for the bag.
  Guide their thinking with the following questions:
    How can you put the bag to other uses? (**put to other uses**)
    What if you could make the bag larger? (**magnify**)
    What if you could make the bag smaller? (**minify**)
    What if you could make the bag out of different material? (**substitute**)
    What if you could cut or tear it into pieces? (**modify**) What can you change? Form? Texture? Shape? Color? Substance? Taste? What could you use it for then? (**modify**)
    What if you could add something to it or combine it with something else? (**combination**)
    What else is it like? What ideas does this give you? (**adapt**)
    Can you rearrange the parts? (**rearrange**) Or can you reverse (turn upside down, backwards or inside out)? (**reverse**)
  After a list of ideas has been generated, ask students to individually choose the three ideas that they would present to a bag manufacturer that has hired them to come up with new ideas to increase their business.
  Post the key words for each question so that students will have these techniques for generating ideas with other projects.

Lesson 5—Inventor's Spotlight
  This lesson may be used several times during the course of study. Its intent is to familiarize students with various inventors, provide a takeoff point for further investigations, and promote evaluation of inventors' contributions. Each spotlight involves a brief report on the background and contributions of an inventor. Basic information about inventors can be found in encyclopedias or reference books on inventors and invention. The instructor may provide students with this information initially, but as students progress through their individual research, they can be encouraged to provide the spotlight.

  Follow up for each spotlight could be one or more of the following questions or projects:
  1. What is one thing you learned about _____?
  2. How did this inventor's contributions change the world?
  3. What would have happened if he/she had not lived?
  4. What things were happening in the world during the inventor's lifetime that helped or hindered his/her inventing?
  5. How did this invention contribute to a better life?
  6. How was _____ like _____ (another inventor)?
  7. Which invention was the most important?
  8. How has this invention changed since the time it was invented? Do you think it will change in the future? How?

9. How did other people (parents, spouses, teachers, siblings) help?
10. What if _____ had been born 50 years earlier?
11. What would have been different if _____ had lived in another country?
12. What is something else about this inventor that you would like to know?
13. What personal characteristics did this inventor have that enabled him to make this contribution?
14. How is this inventor like other inventors we have studied?
    How was he/she different?
15. How has this invention changed our lives?
16. Who else helped?
17. What would he/she be inventing if he/she lived today?
18. If you were in _____ 's shoes, how would you feel?
    What would you do?
19. What circumstances in the inventor's life helped or hindered his role as an inventor?

Lesson 6—What's Needed?

Divide class into small groups. Have each group make a list of inventions or machines that we really need. Then ask them to make a list of inventions or machines that we have that we could do without. Share ideas with the entire class. After all ideas have been shared, decide as a class what five inventions could be easily discarded. Also compile a list of the five most important inventions yet to be invented.

Lesson 7—Attribute Listing

Discuss what an attribute is—a characteristic or function of something. Then ask students to list the attributes of a pencil. Attributes will be things like, "covered with wood, round, straight, used to write with..." Make a list of ideas as they are given. Refer to the list of attributes to brainstorm ways to change a pencil. List all ideas.

As a group list the attributes of a chair. Then have students, either individually or in small groups, use the list of attributes to propose how a chair could be changed or improved. After they have made a long list of ideas, have them choose the best ideas to share with the group orally or incorporate into a drawing of their new, improved chair.

Lesson 8—Forced Relationships

Place an object in the middle of each table. First ask students to discuss in partners how they are like their neighbors. Share ideas with the whole group. Then ask them to discuss how they are like the object in the middle of their table. Share ideas with the whole group.

Introduce forced relationships as a creative thinking technique that forces one to look for similarities and differences between two seemingly unrelated objects. This technique forces us to think beyond the obvious and ordinary to generate new possibilities.

Put the following lists of words on the board:

airplane	tree
peanut butter	pillow
baseball	cup
book	bicycle

First have students to suggest how items in the first list might be related to items in the second list. Then ask students to try to combine each item in the first list with an item in the second list to make some new invention.

Finally give students the task of improving a lunch box. To get ideas for the improved lunch box, they must force a relationship between a lunch box and four of the following items: stapler, paperclip, socks, computer, and jump rope.
They should not just try to attach each item to the lunch box but should think about the attributes of the item and what relationships could exist between a lunch box and this item or its attributes.

Lesson 9—Human Qualities

As a group, brainstorm what human qualities one needs to be an inventor. Keep the list and use as a reference when doing the "inventor spotlights" and the center activity. As information about each inventor is presented, check to see which of the qualities are typified by the inventor. Also add qualities as necessary as evidenced by information about inventors.

Sometime toward the end of the time allocated for studying inventing, ask students to refer to the list (which by now has been refined) and categorize the qualities according to those they think would be useful to them as students and those that they do not feel would be useful in a school setting. Then have them check which qualities they feel that they personally possess and which one they would like to develop to a greater extent.

Lesson 10—Thingamajig

Combine several pieces of junk into one fanciful invention. Show students your thingamajig. Ask them to suggest what it could be or what it could be used for. Encourage a large quantity and variety of ideas.

Divide student into small groups. Give each group a sack full of junk. Ask each group to combine the junk in some original fashion to make their own thingamajig. Upon completion, each group should name the invention and describe its use.

Lesson 11—Combinations

Many inventions are clever combinations of two or more things that are already in existence. Examples of this are the clock radio, moped, combined pen and felt-tip marker, and skateboard.

Ask students to first suggest other examples of inventions that are combinations of two things. Then ask them to suggest things they could combine with each of the following to make new, useful inventions.

towel	chalkboard
piggybank	frisbee
belt	backpack

Have students choose the idea they like the best and create an advertisement for the new item.

Lesson 12—Everyday Things

Often inventors get their ideas by looking at everyday things and seeing possibilities for improvements or new applications. Indeed, some theorists define creativity as seeing everyday things in new ways.

Select an everyday object to study and do the following:

- *List the attributes.*
- *List the common uses.*
- *Find out how it works.*
- *Find out how it is made.*
- *Rate how valuable it would be to someone on a deserted island, someone living in a large city, someone on their way to the moon, or a primitive tribe.*
- *What problems are associated with it?*
- *List other things that are like it.*
- *What questions can you ask about it?*
- *What are some unusual uses for it?*
- *How can you make it more appealing to a _____ ?*
- *How can you change what goes on the inside?*
- *How can you change what goes on the outside?*
- *Can you combine it with another object?*

Lesson 13—Other Ways

Inventions are often the result of looking for other ways (usually more efficient, less costly, or faster) of doing things. In this lesson, students are asked to think about how else they could accomplish certain tasks.

Divide the class into small groups. Assign each group a task and ask members of the group to brainstorm other ways that they could accomplish this task. They may begin their brainstorming by listing conventional ways of accomplishing the task, but they should go on to creative, original ideas. They should be encouraged to think of wild ideas as well as sensible ideas, as the wild ideas could trigger other more workable ideas or could be changed in some way to make them workable.

What are all the ways you could:

- *keep a shoe on a foot*
- *keep food from spoiling*
- *lift an object weighing 2000 pounds and move it 10 feet*
- *prevent an egg from breaking when dropped from a height of 20 feet*
- *sharpen a pencil*
- *cut a birthday cake*
- *prevent your dog from going into the street*
- *mix the ingredients for a cake*
- *prevent an infestation of a bug that eats fruit*
- *make a hole in the ground*
- *sharpen a pencil*
- *prevent prisoners from escaping*
- *find out if students had learned what you had taught*

Lesson 14—Graffiti Game

This lesson serves as a review of the study of invention and an opportunity for students to express ideas about creativity.

Divide the class into groups of five or six. Prepare a graffiti board for each group. Cut a piece of large butcher paper or newsprint so that each board measures approximately 3 feet by 6 feet. Each board will have the same phrases on it, written in a random fashion with enough room between each phrase so that students can add their own comments. Some possible phrases or quotes are:

To invent is to
Being creative means
Creativity is to inventing as _____ is to _____ .
The greatest inventor is
What we really need to invent is
I think, therefore,
Genius is 99% _____ and 1% _____
Also include several unfinished drawings or the beginning of designs that students can complete.

Students are assigned to groups and instructed that they will be given ten to fifteen minutes to write on their boards. They may respond to the comments and finish the drawings and phrases on the board or they may respond to the comments of their team members. Each team starts with 100 points, and points are subtracted for inappropriate responses and for talking. At the end of the ten minutes, students should circulate to read how other teams answered the same questions. Discuss similarities, differences, and profound statements.

Warm Ups

The ideas in this sections are quick lessons that are designed to focus students' attention on the topic of Inventions and Inventors or to give them opportunities to think creatively about this topic. They may be used at the beginning of a lesson, as students are entering the classroom, or to fill in short periods of time before dismissing class.

1. Where do ideas come from? Tell me two distinct sources.

2. Why do people create things? Give me two different reasons.

3. What would an ideal _____ be like?

4. What are some inventions we really need?

5. What are some inventions we could do without?

6. What are some problems that need solutions?

7. What invention best typifies you?

8. How are you like Edison? Name two common characteristics.

9. How is a tea pot like a cricket? Name two different ways.

10. How could you use the idea of "bees" to come up with ideas to improve patio furniture?

11. How many different ways could you finish this sentence:
"Inventors are like . . . because . . ."

12. What other words come to mind when you think of the word "invent?"

13. Think of an invention that has significantly changed our lives. Show us this invention without making any sound.

14. Here's a lump of imaginary clay. Use it to make an invention that will solve a problem in your home or school.

15. Think of new names for a cereal made out of seaweed.

16. What are some new uses for a _____ .

17. How is a _____ like a _____ .

18. What advice would you have for the leaders of an emerging nation that wanted to encourage more inventions from its residents? Limit your advice to a 10-word message.

19. If you could be an invention, what would you be? Why?

20. In what ways might we improve _____ ?

21. In what ways might we use _____ ?

22. What are all the different ways we could _____ ?

23. What would you like to tell the inventors of today?

24. Suppose _____ didn't exist. How would things be different?

25. How does _____ compare to _____ ?

Learning Centers

Super Machine

Provide several pieces of white 8½" × 11" paper along with the following directions.

Super-Machine — A new kind of dominoes
Draw your version of a super-machine.
Your drawing must take up the entire piece of paper and be able to be joined to either end of the supermachine that has been created by other people.
Make your drawings original, detailed, and neat.
When you are finished, put your name on the back of the drawing and tape it (along the back side) to one side of the supermachine that has been drawn by other people.

When all drawings are joined together, you will have a long mural-life drawing of a machine. Each section should fit with the ones next to it.

Matching Game

Make cards that have the name of an invention on one card and its inventor on another card. Write numbers in the corner of each card so that each inventor-invention pair has the same number.

Students take the deck of cards and turn them face down on a desk. They then take turn turning over two cards. When they can turn over two cards that match (an invention and inventor) they place the pair in their pile. The person with the most pairs at the end of the game wins.

Examples of cards would be:

1 Thomas Edison	1 electric light bulb
2 Wilber and Orville Wright	2 airplane
3 Johann Gutenberg	3 printing press

See list at the end of the book for other combinations.

Categories

Make several cards out of tag board or other heavy, durable paper. Write one of the following headings on each card.

Inventions that were "premature"
Inventions that were "mistakes"
Inventions that are especially beneficial to people
Harmful inventions
Inventions that were a result of teamwork
Inventions that made BIG changes in the world
Inventions that are needed for the future
Inventions that brought people closer together
Small inventions that made a big difference

Laminate cards and attach the following instructions:

Research information about inventions. When you find an invention that will fit into one of these categories, write its name on the appropriate card with the special marking pen.

Things To Do With Junk

Provide students with a box of "good" junk. Also provide cards with the following instructions:

Junk Card - 1
1. Choose at least 10 items from the box.
2. Arrange the items in some sort of a logical group or sequence.

Junk Card - 2
1. Choose two things from the box.
2. List all of the ways they are alike and ways they are different.
3. Think of a new invention you could make by combining the items or by changing one item to include one attribute of the other item.

Junk Card - 3
1. Choose one thing out of the box.
2. List all of the attributes, uses and features of your item.
3. Suggest ways you could change this thing or use it in a new way.

Junk Card - 4
1. Select ten different things from the box.
2. Make as many of the following things in one hour as you can:
   a) something useful in measuring
   b) something used for communication
   c) a trap for a pest
   d) something useful in a classroom
   e) some kind of shelter
   f) a container for mud
   g) a plaything for a small child
   h) something that can sail through the air for 15 feet
   i) something that can spin
   j) something that represents you
   k) a musical instrument

Time Line

Make a long strip of paper that is 6″ wide and as long as is necessary to accommodate the time scale you choose. Make a straight line along the length of the strip and mark off time intervals of every 50 years beginning with 3,000 BC and continuing to the present. Instruct students to mark the date of inventions on the time line at the appropriate place.

After dates of invention have been added to the time line for about two or three weeks, post the time line and discuss when most inventions were invented and why most inventing took place during these times.

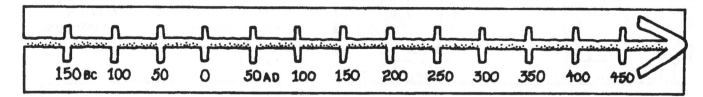

Connections

Divide a piece of tag board into squares. Cut out pictures of several different objects and glue each one into a square. You should have at least twenty pictures. Provide small markers in two different colors. Write the following directions for the game.

This is a game for two players. Each player should choose a color of markers. The first player tries to make a connection between any two pictures by naming the two objects pictured and telling how they are related. You can say things like, "they are both containers, they are made from the same materials, they are both alive, they can both be found in a bedroom, etc." If a connection can be made, a marker is placed on both pictures. The next player must make a connection between the last object named and any other object that does not have a marker on it. If a connection can be made, a marker is placed on the object that does not have a marker on it. If a connection cannot be made, the player must pass. The person who has captured the most objects is the winner.

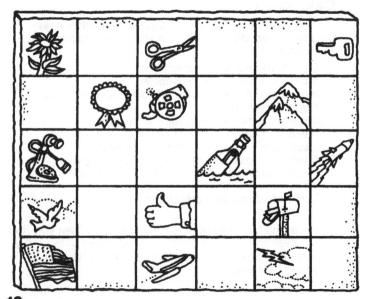

Invention Quilt

Provide students with squares of white paper (approximately 7" × 9"). Each student should choose a different invention. On the top portion of the paper, they should make a drawing of the invention. On the bottom, they should write the name of the invention, the date of invention and a brief historical account. When squares are finished, mount each one on a different color of construction paper and tape them together to form a quilt. Hang in the classroom or in the hall for all students to read.

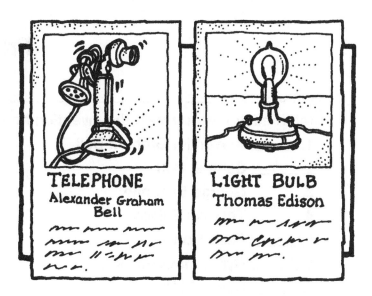

Headlines

Tack several pieces of newsprint on a bulletin board. On each piece of paper, write some headlines from newspapers of the future that deal with invention events. Provide students with pieces of paper to write the news articles to accompany each headline. They may also draw a picture to go with the article. As articles are written, they are mounted under the corresponding headlines. When you are finished, you should have several pages of a newspaper of the future. Some possible headlines are:
- *Invention Aids Blind*
- *Revolutionary New Material*
- *Invention Speeds Communication*
- *Artificial Body Parts Improved*
- *New Hope for Terminally Ill*
- *Inventor of the Year Award*
- *Car of the Future, Here Today!*
- *New Invention Makes Housework Easy*
- *New Process for Recycling Garbage*
- *The Latest Computer Developments*
- *The Invention Everyone Hoped For*
- *Invention Offers Hope for Starving Nations*

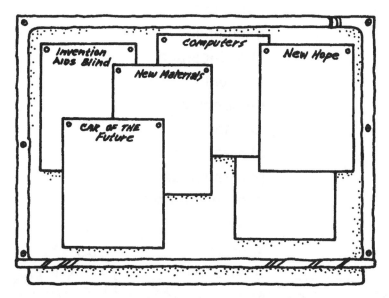

Pretest

Name_____

Match each inventor with the invention he invented.

1. _____ Alexander Graham Bell	a) laser
2. _____ Samuel Colt	b) light bulb
3. _____ George Eastman	c) paper
4. _____ Thomas Edison	d) computer
5. _____ Elias Howe	e) printing press
6. _____ Cyrus McCormick	f) camera
7. _____ Samuel Morse	g) steam engine
8. _____ Kellogg brothers	h) telegraph
9. _____ James Watt	i) airplane
10. _____ Elisha Otis	j) telephone
11. _____ Johann Gutenberg	k) phonograph
12. _____ Eli Whitney	l) cereal
13. _____ ancient Chinese	m) cotton gin
14. _____ Robert Fulton	n) wheel
15. _____ Wright brothers	o) revolver
16. _____ Charles Babbage	p) steamboat
17. _____ Isaac Newton	q) sewing machine
18. _____ ancient Asians	r) elevator
19. _____ Theodore Maiman	s) reaper
	t) telescope

Put these inventions in order. Put a 1 by the invention that was invented first, a 2 by the next invention to be invented and a 10 by the most recent invention.

_____ light bulb	_____ sewing machine
_____ laser	_____ match
_____ wheel	_____ zipper
_____ radio	_____ typewriter
_____ submarine	_____ telephone

1. Define invention _____

   _____

2. One human quality or characteristic that an inventor should have is _____

   _____.

3. What, in your opinion, are some of the most important inventions that have been invented so far? _____

   _____

4. Write as many answers to this question as you can think of:

   Where do ideas come from?

   _____

   _____

   _____

   _____

5. What is your definition of the word "creativity?" _____

   _____

Uses

Lucky you! You have just won fourth prize in the Local Association of Builders (LAB) yearly raffle. You have won a brick. Now you have to decide what you will do with the prize.

How many different uses can you think of for a brick? List as many as you can.

_____   _____
_____   _____
_____   _____
_____   _____
_____   _____
_____   _____

How many more uses can you think of if you can change the brick in some way—make it smaller, make it larger, break it into pieces, or combine it with other bricks or other things?

_____   _____
_____   _____
_____   _____
_____   _____
_____   _____
_____   _____
_____   _____
_____   _____

Unusual Uses

List several uses (usual and unusual) for these items.

scissors

_____

_____

_____

_____

_____

_____

_____

_____

paper clip

_____

_____

_____

_____

_____

_____

_____

_____

feather duster

_____

_____

_____

_____

_____

_____

_____

_____

skateboard

_____

_____

_____

_____

_____

_____

_____

_____

Assessing Attributes

Name _____

Attributes are the characteristics and functions of an item. Attributes could be the size, shape, appearance, weight, purpose, use, or material of construction of an object.

By looking at the attributes of something, we are often able to see new ways that we can change it to make a new, improved version.

What are the attributes of a backpack?

_____

_____

_____

_____

_____

_____

_____

_____

_____

_____

_____

Think about some of the attributes you have listed. How could you change a backpack by changing the attributes?

_____

_____

_____

_____

_____

Which change do you think would be the most useful and why?

_____

_____

Using Attributes

Make a list of all the things you can think of that have the following attributes.

Things that are soft	Things that are sticky
_____	_____
_____	_____
_____	_____
_____	_____
_____	_____

Things that go around   Things that grow

_____	_____
_____	_____
_____	_____
_____	_____
_____	_____

How could you combine two things from your lists to make a new, useful object?

Combine _____ and _____ to make a _____

_____

The function of this invention would be _____

_____

Making Changes

Name _____

You have just found a magic lamp that will enable you to perform magical transformations. With these abilities, you are able to improve things by making changes.

Think about what ways you could improve shoes if you could perform the following changes.

1. Increase in size or quantity _____

_____

2. Decrease in size or quantity _____

_____

3. Substitute something _____

_____

4. Modify in some manner_____

_____

5. Combine with something else _____

_____

6. Rearrange or reverse _____

_____

7. Adapt for another use _____

_____

Something Extra

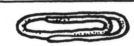 

Use these transformations to think of ways that would could improve one of the following:

sweater   paperclip   hammer   tack

Imagination Exercise

Name _____

Inventors often get their ideas by looking at a common object and thinking about what else it could be besides its present function and form.

Here are sketches of cups. Draw details to make each one into something different. Be original and try to think of unusual modifications for the cups.

Using What You Have

Name _____

Inventors are limited by the materials that are available. Looking at the materials that are available often makes an inventor think of new applications.

How many different ways could you use a piece of string, a piece of paper, and a pencil to measure either length, weight, capacity, or time?

_____

_____

_____

_____

_____

_____

_____

How many different ways could you use a cup, a comb, a length of chain, and a fork to make sounds?

_____

_____

_____

_____

_____

_____

_____

_____

Forced Relationships

Name_____

Often it is possible to think of improvements for one item by thinking about another item.

What ideas come to mind for changing or improving shoes when you think about each of these things?

a computer   a Monopoly game ®
peanut butter   a garden hose
a bumble bee   a weed

Write all of your ideas here.

_____

_____

_____

_____

_____

_____

_____

_____

_____

_____

I think my best idea is _____

_____

Doing the Job

Name _____

Most inventions are practical and useful. They usually try to simplify a task, reduce the work, or accomplish more work with the same input of energy.

Make a list of tasks that you have to do.

_____   brushing teeth _____

_____   _____

_____   _____

washing dishes _____   _____

_____   pulling weeds _____

_____

Choose one of these tasks and think about what you could do to make it easier or more efficient to do this task. List all of your ideas.

_____

_____

_____

_____

Choose the best idea and describe how it would work.

_____

_____

_____

Sorting Steps

Name_____

Here are the steps that most inventors go through when they are inventing. Put the steps in order by putting a 1 before the first step, a 2 before the second step, and so on.

_____ **Distribution** - find people who will support this idea or a way of selling the idea to the public

_____ **Define the problem** - decide what needs to be solved

_____ **Redefine the problem** - based on new information, what needs to be done

_____ **Assess present situation** - decide what is being done and what already exists, review all relevant information

_____ **Brainstorm** - think of as many ideas as possible

_____ **Experiment** - test to see how idea(s) works or if it meets the necessary criteria

_____ **Analyze** - List criteria and use criteria to select which idea(s) will best solve the problem

_____ **Predict consequences** - decide if this is worth pursuing—who will use it? What might go wrong?

If you write the letters that belong with the number in the order that they appear above, you will have the name of a very famous inventor.

1	2	3	4	5	6	7	8
A	D	E	I	O	S	N	T

____ ____ ____ ____ ____ ____ ____

How It Works

Choose an invention that you find particularly interesting. Find out how this thing works. Use the space below to make a diagram of the invention. Below the diagram, explain how the invention works.

_____

_____

_____

I found out how this invention works by ☐ reading a book ☐ dissecting the invention
☐ asking someone ☐ other _____

What Would It Look Like?

Name _____

Use your imagination and think about what each of these inventions would look like. Then choose one invention and illustrate it in the space below.

a rib tickler

a transaquatic supertrain

an envelope licker

a doughnut duster

an automatic fly killer

an egg sizer

a sediment scoop

a mess picker-upper

Imagineering

Name _____

What could this invention be? Why would people want it?

Draw the inside workings of this machine.

Tell what things you could put into this invention and what would come out.

_____

_____

_____

_____

Something extra:
Write a commercial that will convince people that they should have one of these in their homes.

Invention Categories

Name _____

For each category, name at least one invention that has been developed in the last 50 years and one invention that you would like to see invented in the next 50 years.

Category	Last 50 years	Next 50 years
Engineering		
Food Preparation		
Energy		
Transportation		
Communication		
Farming		
Medical		
Home		
Office		
Recreation / Toys		
Personal		
Entertainment		

Catalog Combinations

Name_____

Select two pages at random from a mail order catalog.

Select any two items from each page.

Write the names of these items in these spaces.

_____

_____

Think about how you could combine two of these things into a new invention. Draw a picture of your new invention.

Name of the invention _____

Description of what the invention does_____

_____

_____

Creative Combinations

Name_____

Often it is possible to invent useful, new products by combining two or three common objects.

List three things that are examples of two distinct objects being combined to make a new object.

1._____

2._____

3._____

Here is a list of five objects. Choose five other objects and write them on the blank spaces.

write your objects here

bike   _____

ball-point pen   _____

baseball hat   _____

wagon   _____

knife   _____

Try combining each object in the first list with each item in the second list. What ideas for new inventions are suggested by each combination? Write your ideas here.

_____

_____

_____

_____

_____

Choose the idea you like the best and describe what this new creative combination would be like.

The idea I like the best is _____

This would be an object that would_____

_____

_____

On the back of this paper, draw your creative combination.

Unfinished Work

Name_____

You have just stumbled on the remains of a partially completed invention. The inventor apparently gave up before finishing the invention. Finish the invention by drawing in all the missing parts.

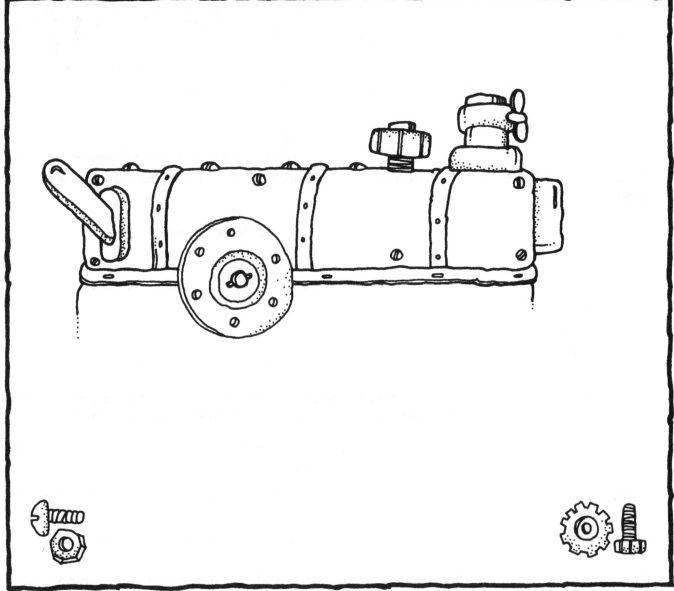

What is the name of the completed invention and what does it do?

_____

_____

_____

_____

Concoctions

Name_____

Here are some word roots and their meanings

tele - distant	**aquatic** - water	**scope** - viewing instrument
trans - across	**macro** - large	**photo** - light
sub - under	**terra** - land	**script** - writing
super - over	**graph** - drawn	**sonic** - sound
vision - seeing	**kinetic** - motion	**micro** - very small

Use these word roots to make your own concoctions. You may add other words if you need to. Describe what each concoction would do.

Example

subaquaticgraphoscope - This is an instrument that will enable people to read or view maps, graphs, and drawings while under water. This device will be very helpful to scientists who are mapping the ocean floor.

1. _____ - _____

   _____

2. _____ - _____

   _____

3. _____ - _____

   _____

4. _____ - _____

   _____

5. _____ - _____

   _____

Choose your best concoction and draw a picture of it on another piece of paper.

The Big Ten

Name_____

What are the greatest inventions of all time? Choose the ten inventions that you think are the greatest. For each invention, tell why you think this invention is important.

1. _____   _____
                            _____

2. _____   _____
                            _____

3. _____   _____
                            _____

4. _____   _____
                            _____

5. _____   _____
                            _____

6. _____   _____
                            _____

7. _____   _____
                            _____

8. _____   _____
                            _____

9. _____   _____
                            _____

10. _____   _____
                            _____

Headline

Name_____

Choose one of the following headlines and write the news story that gives all the facts.

Edison Electrifies Lighting
Light Forms Laser
Transistor Replaces Vacuum Tube
Atomic Power Unleashed
Television Promises New Horizons
Cotton Gin Revolutionizes Agriculture
Fulton's Folly
Tom Thumb Chugs Along
Telephone Will Replace Telegraph

_____

_____

_____

_____

_____

_____

_____

_____

_____

_____

_____

_____

_____

_____

_____

_____

_____

Charting Inventions

Name_____

Use the names and inventions below to complete this chart. In the first column is the name of an inventor. In the second column is the name of his invention. Leave the last column blank until after you have finished the chart.

Inventor	Invention	Importance
Benjamin Franklin		
	sewing machine	
Benz and Daimler		
Robert Fulton		
	radio	
Samuel Morse		
	airplane	
	atomic reactor	
Wilheim Roentgen		
	television	
	phonograph	
Isacc Newton		
	electric lightbulb	
Robert Goddard		
	telephone	

liquid-fueled rocket, steam boat, gas-powered automobile, Thomas Edison, Elias Howe, bifocals, Thomas Edison, Wright brothers, telegraph, Alexander Graham Bell, x-ray, Lee deForest, reflecting telescope, John Baird, Enrico Fermi

In the last column, evaluate how important each development has been. Make your own system of codes and use it to indicate your evaluation.

You, the Inventor

Be an inventor! Invent something new and unique!
Use this form to describe your invention.

Name of inventor _____

Name of invention _____

Description _____
_____
_____
_____

Purpose _____
_____

Who will use this? _____
_____

Why is it needed? _____
_____

How does it work? _____
_____
_____
_____

Diagram of invention - Use another piece of paper to make a diagram of your invention.
Label all important parts.

Planning Sheet for Report on an Invention

Name _____

Invention _____

Date of invention _____

Name of inventor _____

Important contributions that lead to the invention _____

_____

_____

_____

How the invention changed the world _____

_____

_____

Why the invention is important today_____

_____

_____

_____

How it works _____

_____

_____

_____

_____

Other topics to research and include in your report:
- Diagram of how the invention works
- How it has changed since it was first invented
- Other inventions by the same inventor
- Forecast for the future of this invention
- Timeline that shows developments that lead up to this invention and subsequent improvements
- List of all ideas or technology that was necessary before this invention could be developed
- Other inventors connected with this invention
- Reasons why the invention is important
- How you could change this invention to make it better

Planning Sheet for Report on an Inventor

Name _____

Name of Inventor _____

When inventor lived _____

Where inventor lived _____

Facts about childhood _____

_____

_____

_____

Training or schooling _____

_____

_____

Jobs the inventor held _____

_____

Important inventions and dates of invention _____

_____

_____

Interesting or amusing facts or stories about the inventor or about how the inventor made his discovery _____

_____

_____

_____

_____

Other topics to research and include in the report:
- How was the inventor helped by other people?
- How was the invention accepted by people at the time it was first introduced?
- Were other people working on the same invention? If so, why did this inventor get credit for it?
- Did the inventor get rich on the invention?
- What important lessons can you learn from this person?

And Now...

Think About:
Is this a good time for inventions?
Who are today's inventors?
What problems are they working on?

Something to do:
Consult a current magazine of science and technology to find out what things are being invented now.

Make a list of recent inventions or inventions that inventors are presently working on.

Put an * by the inventions that you think will make the most significant changes in your life?

Ethics

Think About:
Should inventors be free to invent anything they want to invent?

What if their inventions are harmful to people?

What would be the result of controlling all inventing?

Something to do:
Think about all the different sides of this problem.

Decide how you feel about it.

Write a convincing argument to support your views.

Give examples to prove your point.

Imaginary Inventions

Think about the following "inventions."
What would they look like?
What would they do?
How would you use them?
Are they worthwhile?

Something to do:
Choose one "invention" and draw what it looks like and describe what it does.

Write a users manual.

- audiotelevideoscope
- smackbacker
- sonicwriter

- antiranter
- telebugprotector
- declogger

- tele-o-tally-o-graph
- calcu-cooker

Materials for Making Things

Think About:
Inventors usually have to work with the materials that are available. By studying existing materials and their properties, they often think of new applications or uses for the materials that lead to new inventions.

Something to do:
Choose one list of materials on the back of this card.

Decide what you could make with these things.

Describe (in drawing and/or words) your invention.

Questions for an Inventor

Think About:
How are inventors different from other people?
How are they the same?
How do they feel about their inventions?
If you could meet your favorite inventor, what would you say?

Something to do:
Choose an inventor that you think is especially interesting.

Find out as much as you can about this inventor.

Make a list of five to ten questions you would ask this inventor.

My Own Invention

Think About:
What needs improving?
What needs changing?
What do we really need that does not already exist?
What problems need solutions?

Something to do:
Make your own invention.

Draw a picture of it and describe how it works.

Tell why people will want it.

If possible, make a working model of your invention.

Materials

Set 1
egg beater
roller skate
string
pencil
wooden spoon

Set 2
scissors
baseball
rubber band
box of nails
can opener

Set 3
ballpoint pen
scotch tape
stapler
computer keyboard
picture frame

Set 4
sock
bicycle wheel
piece of cardboard
letter opener
watch

What It Takes

Think About:
What does it take to be an inventor?
Are there certain personal qualities an inventor should have?
What does it mean to be creative?

Something to do:
Make a list of your own "Rules of An Inventive Mind."

Include everything you think is important to do in order to be more inventive and creative.

Present your ideas in a checklist, a poster, or a bulletin board.

Looking Backward

Think About:
What inventions have been the most important to you, your parents, and your grandparents?

Something to do:
Make a list of the five most important inventions that have been developed during your lifetime.

Make a list of the five most important inventions for your parents' lifetimes.

Make a list of the five most important inventions for your grandparents' lifetimes.

Advertisements

Think About:
Once an inventor has completed a successful invention, the job is not over. Now someone (either the inventor or a company that buys the rights to the invention) must sell the invention. This means convincing the public that they need this new thing. This is not always easy to do.

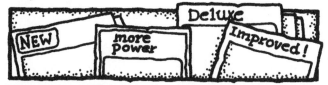

Something to do:
Create an advertisement for a magazine, radio, or television to sell an invention.

Or
Role play a scene where the inventor is trying to persuade someone to buy this invention.

(Your invention can be either a real one or one of the imaginative inventions you have designed as a part of your work in this unit.)

Out of this World

Think About:

Scientists, engineers and inventors are looking into the future, thinking about what new adventures might be possible in the years to come. Many people feel that living and traveling in space is a definite possibility for the future. They are, therefore, planning for the day when humans will live someplace besides on Earth.

Something to do:

Invent something that would be useful in space, on a space station, on the moon, or on another planet.

Write a users' manual to explain everything the owner of this invention would need to know.

Finding Functions

Think About:

Sometimes the ideas for inventions come from thinking about the functions that the inventions would have to perform. To get practice in this kind of thinking, we can think about the functions of some simple everyday items like a pencil, a bathtub, or an egg beater.

Something to do:

Make up a list of functions for one of these inventions:

sneaker tester   backpack stack
current regulator   sound filter
thought director   guzzle gadget

On another piece of paper, draw your invention. Include all the most important functions in your design.

Acceptance

Think About:

What happens to inventions that are not accepted by people?

What are some inventions that were not accepted by people?

What makes an invention valuable and successful?

Why do some inventions fail to gain acceptance?

Something to do:

Find examples of inventions that were not accepted at the time of their invention.

Make a list of conditions you think are necessary for an invention to be accepted.

Inventive Times

Think About:
What times have been most conducive to inventing?
What accounts for these periods of innovation?

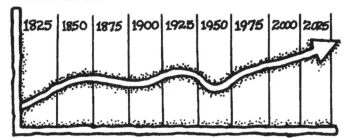

Something to do:
Look at a timeline of inventions.

Make a graph that shows the number of significant inventions in each 25-year increment.

Tell what periods had the most inventions.

Explain why there was more inventing taking place during these periods than during other times.

Improving Inventions

Think About:
Often inventions are improvements of existing items. Small changes or variations can significantly improve items, making them more efficient or easier to use.
What needs improving?

Something to do:
Decide what common, everyday invention you could improve.

List many ideas for improving it.

Choose the best ideas.

Make a poster or diagram that shows your improved version.

Elaborating

Think About:
People often take a simple item and add to it to make new or improved versions. This is called elaborating. When you elaborate you add details, fill in the gaps, build groups of related ideas, or stretch and expand on the basic idea.

Something to do:
Choose a simple item like a pencil. List all of the things people have done to change this item— things they have added to it, ways they have changed the outside or inside, or ways they have combined it with other things.

Make a list of your own ideas to change this item.

Great Moments in History

Think About:

History is full of interesting stories about inventions. There are stories of dreams or observations that lead to breakthroughs, accidents that resulted in innovations, and instances of individual perservance and cooperative teamwork.

Something to do:

Produce and present a "you are there" newscast in which you reenact scenes from the lives of inventors.

Some ideas might be:

Goodyear spilling the compound that lead to the discovery of vulcanized rubber.

Elias Howe explaining his dream that lead to the development of the sewing machine

Alexander Graham Bell's first words on the telephone.

Invention Process

Think About:

What steps does an inventor go through?
Is inventing a random process?
Can people learn to be inventors?
How can the inventing process be applied to solving problems in general?

Something to do:

Make a flow chart that shows the process one would follow from initially thinking about a problem to the final step of selling the invention.

In What Ways Might We

Think About:

While we usually do things in the same, traditional manner, there are many ways of accomplishing everyday tasks. By thinking of different ways of doing things, inventors sometimes think of better ways to do things.

Something to do:

Choose one of the following things and list as many ways as possible to accomplish this task. When you have listed all the usual ways of doing this things, think of usual or creative ways of doing it.

open a can
get from here to there
sharpen a pencil
fasten tennis shoes
entertain a small child
lift a 2,000 pound package

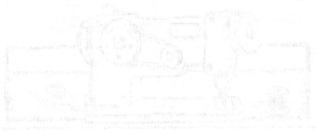

Quotables

Quotes to Think About:
"Invention is 1% inspiration and 99% perspiration."
"Necessity is the mother of invention."
"There's nothing new under the sun."
"If you build a better mousetrap, the world will beat a path to your door."
"The greatest inventions are those inquiries which tend to increase the power of man over matter."

Something to do:
Choose one of these quotes and explain what it means using your own words.

Tell whether you agree or disagree with the quotation. Give examples to back up your opinion.

Write your own "quotable" statement relating to inventions or inventing.

Before and After

Think About:
What circumstances or developments are necessary before invention takes place?
What raw materials must be available?
Do some inventions depend on other inventions? How?

Something to do:
Choose an important invention.
List all the inventions that needed to be developed before this invention could be invented.

List all of the inventions that came after the development of this invention.

Describe how this invention has changed or has been improved since its first development.

Invention Puzzle

Think About:
Who are the most important inventors?
What are the most important inventions?
What facts about inventions and inventors are worth knowing?

Something to do:
Make a puzzle or game that will teach someone about inventors and their inventions.

Give your puzzle or game to a friend to solve.

Ask your friend to evaluate it.

Recombinations

Think About:

One way to come up with new ideas is to take materials or parts that already exist and combine them in new ways. In doing this, you look for ways that you can rearrange the parts, reverse the order, or put the parts to another use.

Something to do:

Take the parts of a bicycle and rearrange them to make something different. Draw your new invention and tell how it works.

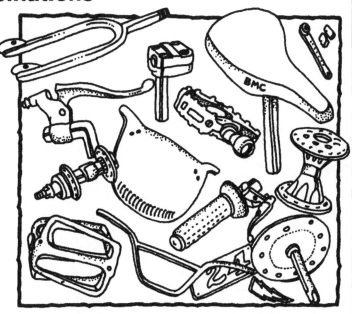

Times of Invention

Think About:

What was the Industrial Revolution?
When did it occur?
Where did it occur?
What inventions were invented then?
Are we in the middle of a new Industrial Revolution?

Something to do:

Find the answers to the questions listed on this card.

Make a list of some of the important inventions that were invented during the Industrial Revolution.

Write a paragraph for a social studies book that tells about the Industrial Revolution.

Help Wanted

Think About:

What personal qualities does someone need to be an inventor?
Do inventors need special training?
What is "the inventive mind?"

Something to do:

Write a help-wanted advertisement for an inventor.

In the advertisement describe what qualities you think are the most important for an inventor.

Needed Now!

Think About:
What problems do we have now?
What things could be improved?
How can inventive minds solve problems?

Something to do:
Make a long list of problems that we now face as individuals or as members of a community or as residents of earth.

Choose five of the problems and describe what kind of an invention would help solve each problem. The inventions can be imaginative, and you may just describe the function of the machine instead of how it works in detail.

Inventor's Award

Think About:
Who was the greatest inventor?
Why was he/she the greatest?

Something to do:
Make an award for the "Greatest Inventor."
Tell who you would give this award to.
Tell why you chose this person.

Rube Goldberg

History:
Rube Goldberg was not really an inventor. He was a cartoonist who drew inventions or machines. These inventions performed a simple task in a very complicated manner.

Something to do:
Study several Rube Goldberg drawings.

Design your own Rube Goldberg machine to do one of the following things.

crack an egg   feed your pet

sharpen a pencil   wake you up

extinguish a flame on a candle

bring in the newspaper

Make a drawing of your invention and explain how it works.

Analyzing an Invention

Think About:

An invention is something that is new and original. Most inventions are attempts to simplify work or accomplish more work with the same (or less) input of energy. Many inventions are merely changes or improvements of existing items.

Something to do:

Choose an invention and do two of the following:

1. Make a chart that shows how it works.
2. Make a timeline that shows how it has developed or changed.
3. Tell what the effects would be if it were to suddenly disappear.
4. Tell how it could be changed to solve a problem that exists in our world today.
5. List ten interesting facts about it.
6. Make a "Yesterday, Today, and Tomorrow" poster that shows how the invention looked when it was first invented, what it looks like today, and what it might look like in the future.

Patent Pending

Think About:

What is a patent?
Where do you get one?
Why do you get one?
How long does a patent last?

Something to do:

Make a flowchart that shows the procedure for getting a patent.

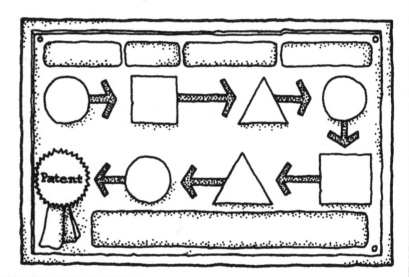

Categories

Think About:

The Patent Office divides inventions into sixteen areas. Some of these categories are transportation, communications, power generation, farming, toys, personal, entertainment, and office. There are, however, many ways to think about inventions—useful, frivolous, mechanical, non-mechanical, life-saving, time-saving, etc.

Something to do:

Find or make a long list of inventions.

Decide on a way to divide inventions into groups.

Use these categories to divide your list of inventions into groups.

Picking the Best

Think About:
What inventions have been the most important?
What makes an invention worthwhile?
Why are some inventions more important than others?
What criteria do you use to determine whether an invention is important or not?
What kind of inventing deserves support from our government?

Something to do:
You have just been appointed as one of the judges for the Invention of the Year Award. Make a list of the criteria you will use to determine which invention should win the award.

List three things that have been invented in your lifetime that you feel meet these criteria and, therefore, should be nominated for the award.

Time for Invention

Think About:
How are inventors influenced by what is happening in society?

Are certain times or certain conditions better for inventing?

What would happen if some inventors had lived at an earlier or later time?

Something to do:
Choose an important inventor.

List other people who were living at the same time and other historical happenings that took place during his/her lifetime.

Explain why you think this was a good time for this inventor to be working on the inventions he did.

Borrowing from Nature

Think About:
The ideas for many inventions came from looking at nature. One example is the cotton gin. The idea for a cotton gin came from thinking about a cat's claws.

Something to do:
Find other examples of inventions that were inspired by nature.

Make diagrams and drawings that show the similarities.

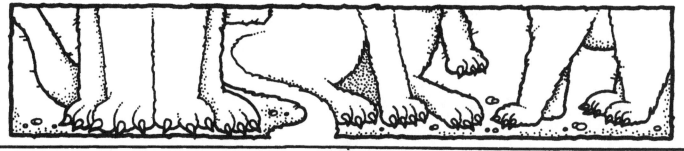

Invention Patent

Patent number _____

The Office of Creativity and Invention is happy to issue a patent to

_____

for the following invention.

Invention name _____

Description _____

_____

The Office of Creativity and Invention finds that this is an original and useful invention. The holder of this patent is the sole owner of rights of production and sales. This patent is good for a period of 9 months or until the end of the present school year.

signature of patent officer _____

Date of issue _____

Official Seal

Inventions Reference List

The following is a list of inventions, inventors and dates of invention for some of the most important or well-known inventions. In cases where the invention was a result of a series of developments by several people, all these have been noted.

Invention	Inventor	Date
Abacus	Chinese	c.500 B.C.
Airplane	Orville and Wilbur Wright	1903
Aqua-lung	Cousteau and Gagnan	1942
Atomic reactor	Enrico Fermi	1942
Automobile engine	Daimler and Benz	1887
Balloon flight	J. Montgolfier	1783
Ballpoint pen	Laszlo Biro	1935
Barbed wire	Joseph Glidden	1873
Battery	Luigi Galvani	1786
(electric)	Alessandro Volta	1800
Bicycle	Karl von Sauerbronn	1816
Braille	Louis Braille	1822
Calculating machine	Blaise Pascal	1642
Camera	Niepce and Daguerre	1822
(Kodak)	George Eastman	1888
(polaroid)	Edwin Land	1947
Cement	Joseph Aspdin	1824
Compass	Chinese	c.1000
Computer		
(digital computing machine)	Charles Babbage	1823
(automatic digital)	Howard Aiken	1944
(electronic)	Eckert and Mauchley	1946
Cotton gin	Eli Whitney	1793
Cyclotron	Ernest Lawrence	1931
Diesel engine	Roudolf Diesel	1897
Dynamite	Alfred Nobel	1867
Electric power system	Westinghouse	1888
Electron microscope	Vladimir Zworykin	1939
Elevator	Elisha Otis	1853
Eye glasses	Italians	c.1200
Fireworks	Chinese	1000
Fluorescent lights	Alexandre Becquerel	1859
Frozen food	Clarence Birdseye	1925
Gasoline engine	Jean Lenoir	1859
Gears	Chinese	c.3000 B.C.
Glass	Asians	c.1500 B.C.
Glue	prehistoric people	
Hearing aid	Miller Hutchinson	1902
Horse shoe	Romans	c.100 A.D.
Ice cream	Romans	c.100 A.D.
Ink	Chinese and Egyptians	c.2500 B.C.
Jeans	Levi Strauss	1850
Jet engine	Frank Whittle	1930
Knife	Stone Age people	
Laser	Theodore Maiman	1960
Lightning conductor	Benjamin Franklin	1752
Linotype	Otto Mergenthaler	1886
Mass assembly method	Henry Ford	1896

62

Match	John Walker	1827
(safety)	Gustave Pasch	1844
Microscope	Zacharias Janssen	1600
Movable type printing press	Johann Gutenberg	1450
	Chinese	c.1040
Money (metal)	Egyptians	c.2500 B.C.
Money (paper)	Chinese	c.1200
Motorcycle	Edward Butler	1885
Nails	Middle Eastern people	c.3000 B.C.
Paper	Chinese	c.100 A.D.
Phonograph	Thomas Edison	1877
Plow (steele)	John Deere	1837
Potato chips	George Crum	1853
Radar	Young and Taylor	1933
Radio(triode)	Lee de Forest	1906
Radio telegraph (wireless)	Guglielmo Marconi	1895
Reaper	Cyrus McCormick	1834
Refrigerator	Ferdinand Carre	1858
Revolver gun	Samuel Colt	1836
Rocket	Goddard	1926
	Chinese	c.1100
Roller skates	Joseph Merlin	1760
Rubber (vulcanized)	Charles Goodyear	1839
Safety pins	Walter Hunt	1849
Safety razor	King C. Gillette	1895
Screw (water raising)	Archimedes	c.200 B.C.
Sewing machine	Elias Howe	1846
	Thomas Saint	1790
Soap	Middle Eastern people	c.3000 B.C.
Steam engine	James Watt	1765
	Thomas Newcomen	1712
Steam boat	Robert Fulton	1787
Submarine	Nautilus	1954
	John Holland	1898
Telegraph	Samuel Morse	1836
Telephone	Alexander Graham Bell	1876
Telescope	Isaac Newton	1608
Television	John Baird	1926
	Vladimir Zworykin	1923
	Paul Nipkow	1884
	Philo Farnsworth	1930
Typewriter	C. L. Sholes	1867
Transistor	Shockly, Bardeen, Brattain	1948
Vacuum cleaner	Cecil Booth	1901
Vaccination	Dr. Edward Jenner	1796
Vacuum tube (triode)	Lee deForest	1906
Velcro fasteners	George de Mestral	1956
Washing machine	Hamilton Smith	1858
Wheel	Asians	c.3000 B.C.
Xerographic copier	Chester Carlson	1948
X-ray	Roentgen	1895
Zipper	Whitcomb Judson	1892

Answers to pretest

1. j   2. o   3. f   4. b,k   5. q   6. s   7. h   8. i   9. g   10. r
11. e   12. m   13. c   14. p   15. l   16. d   17. t   18. n   19. a

1. wheel (3,000 B.C.)
2. match (1827)
3. sewing machine (1846)
4. typewriter (1867)
5. telephone (1876)
6. light bulb (1880)
7. zipper (1892)
8. radio (1895)
9. submarine (1898)
10. laser (1960)

1. Inventions are new, original things or processes that facilitate or make possible things that were previously difficult or impossible. Most inventions are practical attempts to simplify work or accomplish more useful work. (answers will vary)
2. Answers will vary but some possible answers are knowledge, persistence, willingness to work, willingness to take risks, creativity, intelligence or expertise.
3. Answers will vary.
4. Answers will vary be should include the idea of being able to come up with new and original ideas.

Answers to Charting Inventions

Franklin - bifocals
Benz & Daimler - automobile
deForest - radio
Wright brothers - airplane
Roentgen - x-ray
Edison - phonograph
Edison - light bulb
Bell - telephone

Howe - sewing machine
Fulton - steamboat
Morse - telegraph
Fermi - atomic reactor
Baird - television
Newton - telescope
Goddard - rocket